Soil

poems by

Maja Zmyslowski

Finishing Line Press
Georgetown, Kentucky

Soil

Copyright © 2020 by Maja Zmyslowski
ISBN 978-1-64662-312-9 First Edition
All rights reserved under International and Pan-American Copyright Conventions. No part of this book may be reproduced in any manner whatsoever without written permission from the publisher, except in the case of brief quotations embodied in critical articles and reviews.

ACKNOWLEDGMENTS

Thanks to the editors of the following literary journals, where these poems first appeared, sometimes with slight variations:

The Briar Cliff Review: "The Murder Birds of Heron Island"
Mid-American Review: "Me, A Map, Island Bound"—finalist for the 2016/17 James Wright poetry award
North American Review: "The Children We Didn't Have"—finalist for the 2018 James Hearst poetry prize

Publisher: Leah Maines
Editor: Christen Kincaid
Cover Art: Jason Raudebaugh
Author Photo: Emily Apsell, Every Love Photography
Cover Design: Elizabeth Maines McCleavy
Interior Art: Dorota Lagida-Ostling

Order online: www.finishinglinepress.com
              also available on amazon.com

Author inquiries and mail orders:
Finishing Line Press
P. O. Box 1626
Georgetown, Kentucky 40324
U. S. A.

Table of Contents

Baby Beets 1

Me, A Map, Island Bound 3

Orchidaceae 5

The Murder Birds of Heron Island 7

Making Pancakes 8

The Children We Didn't Have 9

Cactaceae 11

Cloud Isles 12

Baltic Amber 13

Sowing 14

Gardeners Who Tend 15

Barren 16

The Wombing 18

Birth 19

I Name My Children after Gods 20

For Ares,
my seedling goddess

Baby Beets

I garden with my hands,
scoop the mineral mud and
earthworms' shit under my nails,
think about smearing it on my face,
the world's cheapest yet richest facial,
much like the natural blush and lipstick
made of juice my grandmother strangled
from a new sugar beet, cut in half, pressing
the menstrual sphere to my cheeks and lips
softly in circles, the Tyrian purple stain sheer
enough for my copper freckles to spy through.
The face of the beet swirled like Jupiter's storm,
and she'd throw it and me into the pot to leech
lifeblood borscht. Now, the eggshell gouged soil
is my own womb, growing dense turnip tumors
and celery cysts. I have harvested plump cherry
tomatoes, burst them between my front teeth,
aiming the launch of golden tadpole seeds
at the oak nursery bed my husband built
years ago, before I even knew how
difficult it would be to make
anything grow.

Me, A Map, Island Bound

The scars on my body run across

my knees, five dime-sized abrasions, earned on a honeymoon
scuba mission chasing puffer fish around the island perimeter.
It was the manta rays that startled us, the first beckoning the second
to waltz beneath like sodden black maple leaves in a whirlpool.

Their wings fluttered through sun rays like polka-dotted umbrellas
straining to open under water. Instinctually, I pulled my knees into
my body, then released them into a tangle of coral. Ribbons of blood
looped through the reef, absorbed by throbbing green anemones.

> One wound wept salt water for five days until it formed
> a starfish crust
> that left behind an imperfection shaped like Oahu when it
> fell away.

Left lower abdomen, five inches across, a collapsed gill,
where a scalpel slid to poke an angry organ, tongs extracting
a bloated puffer fish, plunking it down on a scale to be weighed.
Laying on my back, the scar is colorless, waxy.

> When standing, the fold above it droops over slightly,
> forming a puckered half smile,
> as though my stomach ate a lemon.

Right underside forearm, a crimped band, a leech's purple kiss,
seared into the skin by the top rack of the oven. I had set out to
bake my husband's favorite meal—tuna noodle. As I scooped
the dish out of the heat, I rested my arm on the metal until

a sharp lick summoned a glossy pink slug to writhe on my skin.
The puffy burn glowed from within, milky liquid straining
against blistering canvas. It's a noticeable, nudibranch scar,
often inspiring the question, *What happened there?* I usually

just smile and say, *Well, he said it was a* nice-but-salty *casserole.*
When I touch it now, the bulge dimples, a beached jellyfish.

Left side of chest, under ribs, a crushed giant urchin.
The closer he got to leaving, the more turquoise his eyes shimmered,
like the waters of Hawaii, where he would float shoulder deep,
buoyed by the salt and laugh as seaweed flirted with his heels.

> I often wish he had died there, pulled under
> by a current moving much too fast
> for the pace of the islands, so that whenever I returned,
> I would feel his bones scrape my feet like coral.

Orchidaceae

I name all the orchids ever given me after goddesses.
Hera, champion of childbirth and family, lists away from
the hospital window,

insulted by the spring day as I lay shivering post dilation and curettage.
She is puce in color, like the French *puce* alluding to the stain

      a crushed flea yields on a bedsheet.

Her thick leaves reach toward me in the shape of an embrace,
and I forgive the braying woman in the next room
for her healthy delivery.

A violet cockleshell orchid came to me after grand-mère passed
unwillingly, just as Persephone rattled against the lowering chariot.

      And so, the flower was named.

The inflorescence droops like a limp ballerina, the chartreuse leaves
form a cradle should sepals fall. She turns her speckled lips toward me

in approval when I blow to cool the sorrel soup on my spoon or dust
angel wing pastries with a blizzard of powdered sugar,

      as grand-mère taught me.

Calliope is a green moth orchid that arrived on my birthday,
a muse to attract words like lusty bees.

I pluck a petal for inspiration and place it on my tongue
like a Communion wafer
to leach sage spores into my bloodstream.

She is my favorite, a living totem of rosary wishes
being screamed into notice,

each petal a period, a question mark,

    a beginning.

The Murder Birds of Heron Island

Those were the pretty years.
When my skin and hair shone without the desperate
nightly slathering of coconut oil. When a man ate
freshly cracked crab out of my hand, sucking
to intercept the clear brine rivulet circling my wrist.

How is it that we watched a hundred thousand turtles
be born, rushing the sea at 2am, yet we can't agree
on who gets the mattress in the guest bedroom?
Him shooing the murder birds away from the tiny
wobbling shells was the same scooting motion
he made when it was decided I would leave our house.

What do I take, besides the cactus we planted as a sentry
for our first home? We had named the desert ranch house
Palm Sway as though it were a sugar cane estate,
and the half acre lot was our island. I could still see
the coffee table-sized mother turtle in the foyer,
laying freckled eggs that ping-ponged toward the den.
But darling, I wanted to say, and point out the manta rays
flopping in the kitchen sink, the starfish pulsating in the pantry.

We never saw a heron on the island, and I believe
it's because the nightly screaming of the murder birds
cut through the focus one might need to build a nest.
So, I'm not surprised when I wake at our house
to hear that avian yelping at 2am, see his eyes
like crests of waves breaking, the ebb and flow leaving foam
in his lashes, brimming his sheer moon jelly lids.

I bet the saliency of his tears is higher
than the waters of the Great Barrier Reef.
One glides to a puddle in the fissure of his collar,
a melted nickel sparkling in moonlight,
illuminating the raft we lay on, shadows all
around us. I wonder why we can't hear the ocean,
when it's only six hundred miles away.

Making Pancakes

I feel like getting fancy today, deciding on whole grain batter
studded with rich
cacao nibs, sprinkled pomegranate arils,
a fat dollop of cream.

I spent months filling the vessel of my body with the bounty of a
thousand gardens
but it remained a vacant arc
awaiting rain.

I whip   with purpose,   each stroke a prayer,
    fold   hard crests   of   egg whites
                    into the beige sea,

                               plop a   ladleful
onto the griddle   and wait,   fingertips
            tracing the plane of my stomach
      where a plump hill   of a belly once   rose.

I miss it tremendously, the hollowed pears of my hands
now empty of flesh
and child alike, but the pancakes are bubbling and the tines
of my fork are sharp.

The Children We Didn't Have
for Teddy & Maggie

For the front yard of our first home you bought
Cephalocereus senilis, an Old Man Cactus,
his hairy white body full of sign language,
one arm forming a question mark,
another, an impressive phallus
that perverted the Santa Claus hat
we placed on his spikey crown
during a 73°F December in the desert.
I named him Clint and you didn't ask why,
just said he looked more like a Theodore
to you, and I didn't ask why.
Two parched summers later, I left
and moved to the coast with him
buckled in the front seat.
I thought you'd find it funny
if I sent you a picture of the cactus
nestled at the base of a pier, waltzing
with the fog, his limbs no longer a confused
seduction but open to the sea, welcoming
brave sea birds to alight on his thorns
already softened to the brackish air.
You thought I'd find it funny
when you sent me a picture
of Mammillaria haniana, the Old Lady Cactus,
that you had planted in the void.
You named her Ada, most likely
after the woman whose stillborn baby
you delivered, later telling me it all
went swimmingly, though I knew otherwise
by your face, and I hadn't the heart then
to tell you I'd miscarried again,
just like I wouldn't tell you now
that the cactus looked like a Margaret to me,
her tiara of jellyfish pink flowers
blooming against the monsoons.

Cactaceae

A cactus has a thousand lives
appearing dead
rolled in on itself
with soft rotten pears
crumbling brown skirt
and broken thorns.
To quote Helena Rubenstein,
there are no ugly women
only lazy ones,
but I am lazy and
this cactus is ugly
and not at all
low maintenance.
I aim a hatchet
at its base, daring it
to shudder but it
just stands there
parched and stoic
too proud to ask for water.
Let's start over,
I tell it and it just shrugs
so, I know it's pissed
but willing.
I trim its dead edges
pluck moldy thorns
snip off spoiled fruit
and ply it
with mineral water.
I do this for months
until it stops scowling
and lifts its head
to puncture the clouds.

Cloud Isles

                    a scientist in love
             an atom's disposition changes upon observation,
             so why doesn't yours, when I look at you?

    soiled sunflower
dark cumulus face crowned
with dandelion flames.
                                        god slurps
                 he uses the ladder of my DNA like a straw, sips up
                 summer fruit soup, blackberries for a bluebird.

                            mourning an oyster
                 when oysters stop making pearls,
                       who will mourn but the world?

    an imploding bomb
the delicate fuse of their hands
holding together the charge.

                           the waltz
               his hand settles in the scoop of her back
                     like a fetus in ripening love.

Baltic Amber

I watch with delight as my date stirs
his stiff drink with a knife, like my father always did,
and I know instantly that I love him.

My father's tumbler was home to a carroty whiskey,
liquefied Baltic amber, like the glass honey stones I now
wear around my neck—cleansing totems that scrub

my throat and kidneys clean. I inherited his eyes,
prisms of moss and ochre within raw ancient gems.
I inherited every stone around my neck.

I look at the man across from me, his ice tinkling,
and crave salted cucumbers and smoked fish
sold by pickled sailors off coastal Gdansk.

Every pebble I collected on that beach held bits
of my father suspended: nail clippings
from his ring finger and big toe, a cloud of his breath

shaped like a strawberry, a blade of bison grass,
a beetle plucking the harp of his eyelashes—
tiny yellow heartbeats warming the resin.

Amber smells of pennies, burnt caramels and tomato vines.
Each inhale is a cradlesong, each exhale an omen.
My date inspects the center stone, takes a sip

of his drink and asks me what's inside. I say it's curled
strips of spliced orange rind, though magnified,
anyone can see it's a double helix.

I'd tried to rip it apart like sour rainbow candy rope,
twist it into a balloon goose, one incapable
of drilling into cork, but it twined together

like the moon lifting the sea's baptismal gown,
revealing my stone eggs on the shore,
no other sound but ice.

Sowing

I spoke a wish to a dead starfish and buried
it inland away from the tide and the sand.

It must've reanimated itself, shuffling from
its burial place back into the brine

and relayed my wish to a whale who later
beached itself in earnest effort to convey

the wish to a gull who would carry it
skyward where the clouds fattened with

delight at being let in on such a secret,
spilling their rain onto a park and into

a fountain where a penny was flung,
only to be picked up by a man who was

superstitious enough to note the year stamped
on it, which happened to be my birth year,

so, when that man entered a sushi restaurant
and ordered jellyfish sashimi, I watched

him play with that coin, spinning it
to catch the light.

Gardeners Who Tend

I met my love at a sushi bar amidst mouthfuls of orange urchin
that melted like overripe persimmon across my gums.
We spoke of lava rock and sand, speculating what
could possibly grow on Icelandic terrain.

Moments later he dazzled with tales of the island's tallest
mountain, *Hvannadalshnjúkur*, or "angelica valley peak,"
a droplet of soy sauce dangling from his beard
like a tropical icicle.

Weeks later he left a giant box wrapped in shell pink paper
on my first story apartment balcony with eight jars
of pickles inside it, because he knew
I'd prefer them to tulips.

Months later, on vacation, I saw him whispering to the water
in the deep end of the pool. Eavesdropping revealed he was lecturing
a bee on proper aquatic survival techniques before scooping
it up and onto the ledge to dry off.

Years later when we bought a house he dug out a rectangular patch in
the backyard that would become a garden, dropping angelica seeds
in my palm and all I could do was wipe the black soil
from his cheek and put it to my tongue.

Barren

                            Like the land
just west of Phoenix,

        where cacti assemble   as if   in a town hall
             meeting, the doctor pronounces

the landscape of my womb   to be   rid dl ed
                                          with tumbleweeds,

       absent
                 of   s e e d s   to disperse.

        I make a list of things I'll do instead

like travel
      and write,   maybe breed garden gnomes,

        and I do those things,   for years.

When my period is late, we don't bat an eye because that's happened before

but   after two weeks   I wonder.

        Drops of pee trickle   off

    the plastic wand ablaze with a plus sign.

        I wave it in front   of my love's eyes,

            my barrenness

                                          rooted.

The Wombing

Ogre tall,
the birch willows of Iceland
grow from black volcanic ash,
highly porous and mineral rich, like
my placental island tethering
our child to the kite of
my womb.

The seedling
within is raspberry-sized,
each drupelet carrying a blueprint
for cowlicked hair, marbled
grey irises, long jumper's
legs and constellations
of freckles.

Icy knoll
of my stomach thawed,
its andosol lining thickens with the
low beat of blood as it carries
the berry through to its
tender ripening and
eruptive harvest.

Birth

I roared her out.

This tiny barnacle unclung
from uterine walls
slid through my pelvis
and tunneled eel-like
toward the horizon
a rudderless ship
swaddled by the sea
her head breached my body
I felt her shoulders
glide from hot
wet to cold wet
seaweed trailing her limbs
I felt her feet paddle
frothing the foam
that soiled the floor
drawing air to
gulp a fish's breath
she shrieked like a gull
and I, emptied of brine
reached out to catch
her moon jelly skin
moist on my chest
the umbilical anchor roping
her to me still pulsating

still roaring.

I Name My Children after Gods

We name her Ares Elisabeth,
after the Greek god of war and my mother.
Between lashings of milk
and daydreams of who she'll become
we think of who we were before
and wonder if we are worthy of her army.
All the orchids in the house are blushing.
The fish in the aquarium float in formation
as our daughter wails a typhoon
to shake the palms in the backyard.
When I introduce her to the garden,
her legs dangling between my basketed
forearms, the tomatoes darken
to a molten orange the color of raw lava.
The last time I was this happy,
I was marooned on an island
in a snowstorm,
rootless.

Maja **Malgorzata Zmyslowski** is an award-winning writer born in Poland, grown in California and matured in Arizona, harboring dreams of casting an anchor into the forests of the Pacific Northwest. When she's not longing for snow and working on her novel, she's flirting with the summer monsoons, wondering what kind of tea to make. Her poems have appeared in *North American Review, Mid-American Review, The Briar Cliff Review* and *Reed Magazine*. Her flash fiction and other work can also be found online and at *www.majazmyslowski.com*.

www.ingramcontent.com/pod-product-compliance
Lightning Source LLC
Chambersburg PA
CBHW050822090426
42737CB00022B/3475